Prayers

for My People

Ehliyahtsiel

"B Real" da poet

Prayers for My People © 2017 by Ehliyahtsiel "B Real" da poet

.

For information contact: info@uptownmediaventures.com

Book and Cover design by Team Uptown

ISBN: 978-1-68121-081-0

First Edition: November 2017

Sankofa
Freedom Press

10 9 8 7 6 5 4 3 2 1

Dedicated to my mother who taught me so very much. I miss her, but her beauty will always be with me. I love you mom!

This book is also dedicated to all the poets and the writers out there who are feeding the artistic, literary, and cultural tributaries of "Black life."

Table of Contents

America, Girl You Slippin'

AMERIKA, AMERIKA GOD SHED HIS LIGHT ON
THEE...

Amerika one hell of of a place

but you ask GOD shed upon you

THEE Heavenly grace

you kill people you steal people

other countries you lay to waste

you come from evil you breed evil

YOU ARE EVIL!!

the time has come again for you to

LET MY PEOPLE GO

free the peoples minds

from your lies and wicked fairy tales

tell the truth about your roots

so i can overstand why it is i do what i do

i am a product of your enviroment

your CULT-TURE

you are the reason i chase my sisters

your material trinkets like a vulture

is how and american lives

love waxed cold

hate created over the years

taught to love the lies and hate the truth

taught to hate and depsise me

and i look just like you

taught to put on a mask a disguise

dont let your real feelins show through

amerika was built on lies

and thats all babylon will ever produce

Amerika girl you slippin

responsible for the lives of many

you got the people stuck

trying to get the latest gigets and gadgets

your programing marinating the minds

of yours his hers and my kind

you dont obey the ways and customs

of THEE true GOD in the Heavens above

you teach more hate to the children

and show less love

took thy lord out of schools

and replaced THEE with blood

now your the chicken head hoodrat

scurvy punk tramp knuckle head rich broad

enter-tainting the minds with

your tell/lie/vision shows

brothers and sisters going at each others throats

on the tv courts

people putting thier bussiness in the streets

on the jerry springer show

i mean how you gone bring me on national

tell/lie/vision

and tell me this women is a man i been kissin

im bout to catch a case wait.....

no i aint cause i wouldnt even show up. anyway

remeber the murders at the Collinbine school episode

well how many copycats you think would have followed

if that story was never told

get right girl you slippin

naked on the beach

plegde ligions to a star spangled banner

is what you preach

what about the convenents we made

family friends my peeps in the streets

i dont care what religion you practice or teach

the covenents pertain to each and every one of us

and our LORD thy GOD is watching every little thing

WE DO

so my people to yourself you got to be true

peace one love from b-real to you

Girl I Wanna Vibe

Girl i wanna vibe off your vibe and you vibe off mine

our anything and everything for ever enter-twined

if im across the ocean sailling down the nile river

my third eye connects with yours and i say come hither

come hither my sweet

thee carob queen of my dreams

ill be your Adam and you can be my Eve

ill be the mind guide we live and you

the protecter of our inner organs our soulsmy heart my rib

i close my seeing eyes contemplate meditate and visualize

you do the same

as we ride the spirit across the plains

they connect come together

our minds our bodies our souls embrace

i open my eyes and see your lovly lovly face

darkbrown mahogany complexion

matching the windows of your soul

i see your full lips yeah girl

you got the kind of beauty that will make a weak man slip

but im strong and you know this if not better get hip

see i aint for them games i leave that for them lames

but anyway back to the vibe you and i on the plains

gliding high descovering the UNI-VERSE

as we rise no need to rush we take our time

circling clouds dodging rainstorms

absorbing feelings never ever felt before

theres a cosmic serge of energy flowing through our heavens

we say a prayer for the sabbaht has just begun

praise the SPIRIT of YAH as we journey up above

soaring never ending heights our Yah minds intact

hey queeen you feelin me picture that

now the season for the planting of our seed is upon us

but just like our THEE CREATOR in the image of THEE are we

so we say be and what it is shall be

a hardy harvest a boy a girl

tummies full of love nurishment and joy

a never ending cycle of life everlasting

no more pain no more sorrow

loving memories of yesterdays and i cant wait until tomorrows

I'm MADD

im madd at ignorant people that wanna stay thay way

im madd at the ignorant words that ignorant rappers
and poets ignorant say

im madd at this wicked ignorantize society im madd

im madd at death im madd at right im madd at left

when i look in the mirror im madd at myself

im madd at what i see im madd at what i hear

im madd at what i thirst and feign

im madd at what i fear im madd

im madd at my sisters

especially the one that wanna be misters

im madd at my brothers on lock-down

with butts full of butter then come round

like aint nothin went down jump off

on the low-down boy

i know you soft im madd

im madd at all you disease infected bucket heads

im madd at the unconscious the walikng dead

im madd at the dope im madd drugs

im madd at the liquor

i aint that madd at the buds

but im madd at that wet water water

im madd at no love im madd

im madd at the stress cause by the wickedness

im madd at the hate that brings on the bitterness

im madd at all my brothers and sisters that really aint
feelin this im madd

im madd at the lies passed off as the truth

im madd at deception the reflection

of evil we do

im madd at him im madd at her im madd at me im madd
you im madd

im madd at greed jelousy and deciet

im madd my people there's no love no unity

only methodical maddness insanity no peace

were all madd

im madd at the snake the serpent the bandit the beast

the imatators of life the good and evil tree

im madd at the father of lies that faggat creaco roman catholic priest

im madd at the pope im madd at false hope im madd at fake gods

argggggg!!! IM MADD

Ehliyahtsiel "B Real" da poet

Message to My Brother, Apologies to My Sisters

i was nutty wild and stuck on stupid/12 years old gettin high playin hooky

from school/ young rookie sleepin through the storm

i thought i was cool tried to tag every piece i could my dudes

showing know respect for the Queen of the earth real rude

now im searching for the treasures she posseses know clue

the Women a gift from our creator

both apart of my brothers and me

she is our rib and we are in the image of THEE

it took me a while to even light-weight wake-up

but peace to them knuckle-heads and bucket heads

cause im no longer stuck/ im not fallin for the pretty smile

the slim waist and the heart shaped butt

i got to work my mind my body my soul my job for YAH

our CREATOR

she got to be my rib by my side watch my back

later for the games female play

games female play

our mother captivated by the serpent in the of eden

all alone/ our farther was somewhere spleein

weak n suspect to the devils evil way

our mother met satan the serpent at the tree of life

AMAZED

it was told from this tree "thou shalt not eat"

the serpent said to Eve just taste you shall see

knowledge and wisdom of I AM who built this kingdom

our mother alone no management

the serpent snake coniving real devilish

in diquise

i forgive you mother Eve for back then all was a suprise

you were the first of our kind to open your eyes

the first WOMEN to know

that your children would learn struggle suffer and then die

you and the first MAN

the first to wittness the death of a Black man

your son at the hand of his own brother man

the world on your consciene and on on your shoulders
Adam

now its up to you to manage your rib and devise a plan

my brothers/you know your girl gone run her mouth

thats one of her treasures/unlock that vault

controled conversation

Ehliyahtsiel "B Real" da poet

MOTHERS

MOTHERS MOTHER MOMMIES

HOW I LOVE THEE / LET ME BE REAL AND COUNT THE WAYS

MOTHERS I LOVE YOU NURTURES YOUR CHILDREN

I REMEMBER AS A CHILD MY MOM WARMED MY HEART

WITH OATMEAL KIND WORDS AND HER BEAUTIFUL SMILE

SHE USE TO SAY

"BABY BREAKFAST IS THE MOST IMPORTANT MEAL OF THE DAY"

HER BEAUTY GLOWED INSIDE OUT

SHOWING ME HER SON WHAT LIFE WAS ALL ABOUT

I MEAN MAMA SPIRIT JUST CAME FORTH

LIKE THE COMING OF THE SPRING /BLOSSOMING

ANOTHER RELM GRACEFULLY AGING BLESSDED BY IAM

IT WASNT ALWAYS SMILES AND GOOD WORDS

"I BROUGHT YOU IN THIS WORLD ILL TAKE YOU OUT"

THATS ONE OF THE PHRASES YOU USE TO SHOUT

I CAUGHT A COUPLE OF BOOKS BOOTS AND HIGH HILL SHOES

TO THE BACK OF MY HEAD

HIDING UNDER THE BED SHE HAD HER BABY BOY SCARED

BUT AFTER EVERY WHOOPIN

HER SMILE AND KIND WORDS RETURN

TALKIN BOUT "THAT HURT MAMA JUST AS MUCH AS IT HURT YOU"

BACK THEN I WAS LIKE YEAH RIGHT

BUT NOW THAT I HAVE A SON

I SEE HOW THAT STATEMENT RINGS TRUE

I LOVE MY MOMS FOR ALL SHE DID AND STILL DO

MOTHERS I LOVE YOU REPLENISHERS OF THE EARTH

FOR NINE MONTHS YOU QUEENS CARRY PROPHETS TO BIRTH

RAISING BOYS TO BE MEN AND LITTLE GIRLS TO BE WOMEN

A MOTHERS LOVE UNCONDITIONAL TRUE TILL THE END

I LOVE YOU MOMMIES

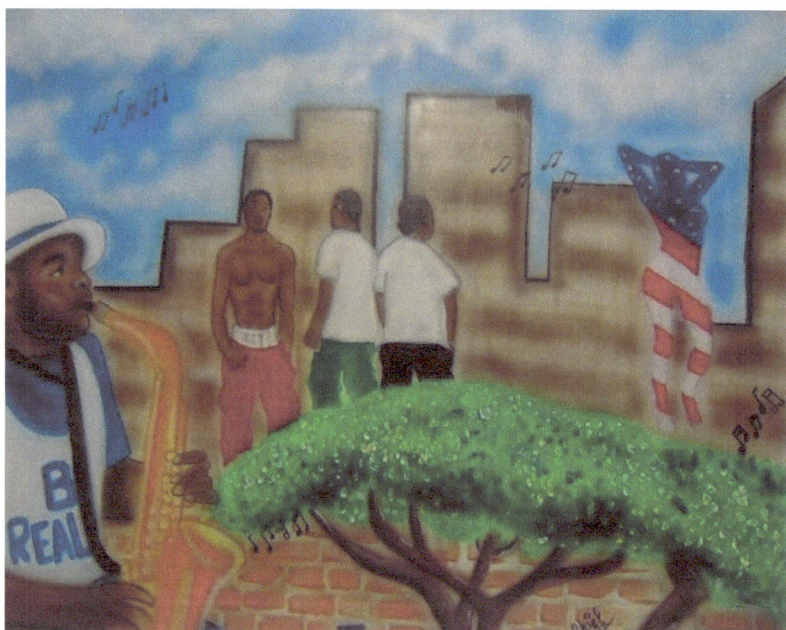

Saggin'

Saggin laggin behide my brothers and sisters

were lost in time trying to find our place

as a people in a world laced with a plethora

of perverted evils good times equated with sex

and nods from needles / the loudest prayinest people on earth

if we could only wake up cathh up with time and be realize our worth

reverse this cursed state of mind were in

THEE CREATOR made us Gods Goddesses

but we keep wanting to be men and women

undivine deaf dumb and blind to the ways of man kind

saggin laggin braggin about what you aint got

put it to a beat and say thats hot

Staring at the Human Ebliss

What is the human ebliss

the human ebliss is the wickedness

that i see every-day every-night

so i take my light and shine bright

for the whole wide world to see

YAH'S Glory

listen listen to the poet tell a story

stairing at the human ebliss

uncontrolled passions of the cursed ones

give me that give me this

i want some money i want some honey

my thoughts are nothing

and everything is HA HA HA funny funny

stairing at the human ebliss

i sit think contemplate then ponder

and i ask myself will i make it from upunder

i wonder

rain stays in my forecast

alone at night i hide from the thunder

i tell the noises and the creepy voices

that i hear in the dark

it just me here and i pray toward the eastern stars

my LORD THY YAH i am your creation

my fathers were Abraham Isacc and Jacob

you made deal with my fathers i am thier seed

dosent the land you gave to them now belong to me

and when i say i and my and me

my brothers and sisters please believe

were all one in the eyes of THEE

so should'nt that land belong to you and me?

well why do we choose to dwell

in amerikinized hell this mind capturing jail

believing in cleverly concocted lies

silly fairytails. well ?

dont answer cause you probably gone tell me

about some reindeer named rudolph or dancer or
prancer

or some rabbit that layed an egg or some fat white man

dressed in red calling it a gift

myth after myth after after myth

stairing at the human ebliss

while being held captive in phyiscal bondage

was very strenuous on the mind the body and the soul

it didnt stop there LORD no no no!!!

the forceful teachings of a new custom

of a new god of a new way

bloodily beaten man women

savagely rape man women and child

my brothers and sisters

take a good look at how we act now

our ways and customs forgotten

our LORD THY only true GOD forgotten

the devil stay plotten

teaching us only to remember

one false prophet

we had and still have the power

to invoke the Spirit of GOD

but we listen to and follow this eruo-gentile peon

making our own lives complicated

so hard so hard

LORD please wake my brothers and sisters

and protect us all from the one called lucifer

that what i say every day as i wake and i pray

i want for my brothers and sisters

what i want for myself

LORD please bring those are righteous

together to share love happiness good health

and wealth

i stair i sit i stair i sit

i stair at the human ebliss

and i wish i wish i wish

for you for me for us to be

as one with THEE

peace

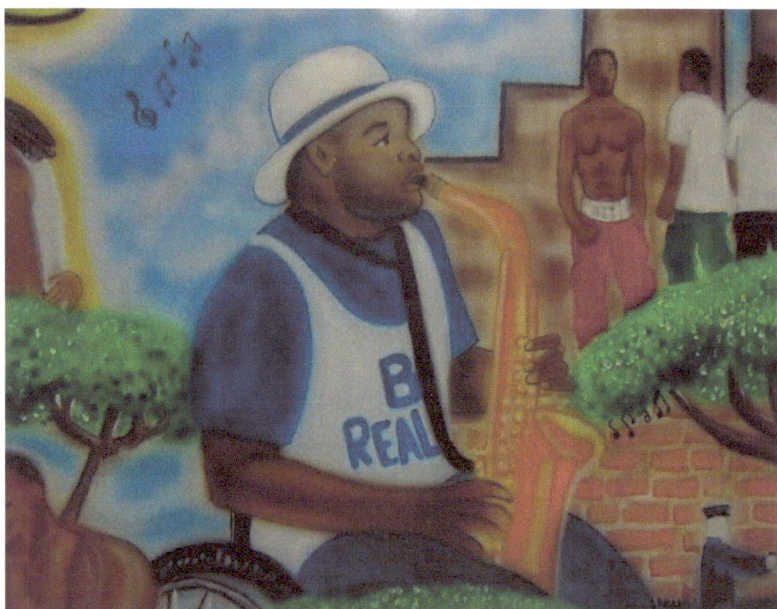

The Best Medicine in the World

(Is Being Real with Yourself)

The best medicine in the world is being real w/
yourself

Come out of denial aknowledge the truth

reject the lying dying life style

this slavemasters taught you

through your ancestrial tree

remember those that came before us and suffered so
that   we

could continue to be/we gotta teach babies

so that ourstory seed of Abraham

dosent become a vanity no more insanity

Lets build a righteous not religeous

world-wide society lets breal and overstand

the concepts of reaping what you sow

lets plant respect for one another and consideration
too

lets plant real joy real smiles on everybodies faces

all races lets plant patients

Lord Yisrael oohh great nation

lets plant beautiful visions in the minds of the people

Creation creating lovly Eden paradise the sequal

no more stairing at the human ebliss no more war going

on

there's no need to call for 911

lets plant love so deep into our D.N.A that every living
thing   on earth
awakes!!!!

at thee appointed time recieving divine undiquised
spirtual
guidance of the mind

everything and everybody doing YAHS thang in harmony
and truth

oh my YAH serving YOU

we'll watch in awe as this YAH SOME plan unfolds

greatful and blessed after each and every episold

no longer a test do good to do right is natural

lets till the earth lets prepare all CREATION for a HEAVENLY   birth

lets drink to our full on truth no more famine no more thirst

every living plant will be beautiful

YEAH

be real beautiful to see and unpolluted you and unpolluted me

a truth undisputed beautiful society

piety growing in the hearts of all man-kinds

every second 24/7 all time devine

the thoughts and images of a breal mind

Unless you be real w/every aspect facet of your life

death will always\ pursue you and youll always ask

why me peace

Ehliyahtsiel "B Real" da poet

The Black Man

THE BLACK MAN ..STONGEST BUT WEAKEST
MAN ON EARTH

the black-man sold traded gave away and robbed

of everything THEE ALMIGHTY CREATOR has givin us

THEE gave us the richest land on the earth

and the average black-man dosent even entertain the
thought

of going back and visiting the land where man was
created

why is so hard for the black-man to embrace the
strongest resource

known to man the black-man wake up black-man

wake up black-man

The Blood that Flows

Ancestor ancient old who knows who knows the blood that flows through viens

pumps the d.n.a of exslaves to my brain

i talk to thoughts old souls

from long ago cry out and tell me stories

as my heart beats a drum

bi dum bi dum bi bi bi bi dum

one thought says with a male lion roar

give me back my brothers

give me back my wife

give me back my father

give me back my life

give me back my GOD

give me back his daughter

im lost im lost

dont leave me for the slaughter

the blood that flows through my brain

is laced with shame chains thunder storms

soak from rain pain

Sam Cooke sang change gone come

yeah thangs done changed

but not for the better

aint no love where i live in this hard knock ghetto

i wanna get over and some breal dont settle

im tired of this damned if you do damned if you dont level

waiting for six feet of dirt a casket and a shevel

how long will it take THEE SPIRIT to rise up for real

how long will it take the people to recognize the true firsr son

YISREAL!! YISRAEL!!

THE BLOOD THAT FLOWS

About the Author

Bryant "B-Real" Wilkerson da poet/musician. Cleveland Born (McDonald House), paralyzed in 1996 in a car accident after being released from prison. He was going through a spiritual war and his prayers led him to poetry.

Twenty years later with, as he puts it, "a clear thought (and peace of mind)," he shares his spiritual growth. The experience "of a man knocked down but not knocked out."

B-Real has performed all over Cleveland including City Hall and the Rock and Roll Hall of Fame. He has performed with the late great Amiri Baraka, he was taught the art of poetry and performed with David (Daveed) Nelson of the *Last Poets*. B-Real prides himself to be counted as one of the *Legacies*, under the tutelage of Cleveland's own *Muntu Poets*.

B Real released a musical spoken word album entitled: *Prayers for My People* in 2017 and continues to be a fixture in the spoken word scene in and around Northeast Ohio and adjoining states.

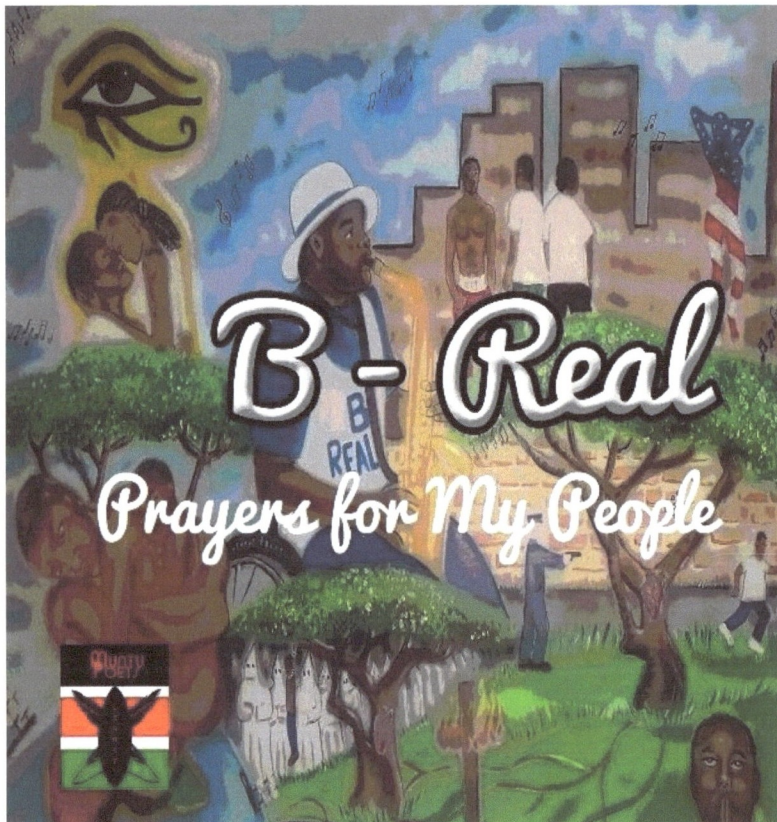

Prayers for My People

Ehliyahtsiel
"B Real" da poet

UPTOWN MEDIA JOINT VENTURES PUBLISHING

Sankofa Freedom Press

www.ingramcontent.com/pod-product-compliance
Lightning Source LLC
LaVergne TN
LVHW072329080426
835508LV00038B/30